Explorers of the Americas

by Michael Sandler

Table of Contents

Introduction

In 1492, Christopher Columbus stepped off a boat and onto an island. He and his crew had left Spain some six weeks before. What was the reason for his trip? He wanted to find a sea **route** to Asia, or as it was called at the time, the Indies. Now, Columbus thought he had done it. He thought the sea route he had taken had brought him to the Indies.

European countries like Spain were eager to find this sea route. European cooks wanted Asian spices to make their food taste better. European kings and queens wanted Asian silk for their royal costumes. For centuries, these goods had reached Europe by land. But land routes were slow, dangerous, and expensive.

By 1492, many people thought the world was round. Columbus was one of them.

 French  Spanish  English  Dutch

1400

1500

1492 Columbus reaches the West Indies.

1497 Cabot reaches North America.

1519 Cortés lands in Mexico and conquers the Aztecs.

▲ A sea route to Asia would give Europe an easier way to get products like spices and silk.

He figured he could reach Asia by sailing west. If this was possible, Asian goods could come to Europe by sea.

Explorers of the New World

Columbus was wrong about where he landed. The islands that he called the West Indies were not part of Asia. They were part of the Americas. These two great land areas, or **continents**, were about to become known as the "New World."

Columbus made four voyages in all. After he died, the Spanish realized his mistake. But they continued to explore the New World. They claimed land, and in time Spain grew rich. Ships loaded with New World goods returned to Spanish **ports**, or harbors.

Other European countries were jealous, so they also sent out explorers. The English, French, and Dutch joined the race to explore the New World.

1533 Pizarro conquers the Incas in South America.

1535 Cartier sails up Canada's St. Lawrence River.

1608 Champlain founds a French city in Canada.

1609 Hudson explores New York's Hudson River.

Peoples of the New World

The Americas were a "New World" to Europeans but not to the people that lived there. Millions of people called the New World home in 1492. The number is probably between 25 and 100 million, but no one knows for sure.

When the explorers arrived, they discovered people living in many different ways. Some, like the Pueblo Indians of the American Southwest, lived in cities. Others were **nomads**, people who moved from place to place to hunt animals and gather food. Millions lived in the great empires of the Aztec and the Inca peoples in Mexico and South America.

▲ In 1507, this map was the first to use the name *America* in the New World.

In this book, you will learn about the explorers of the New World and the people who were already living there. As you read, pay attention to what happened when the two groups met. Notice how the explorers helped European countries become strong in the New World. See how the lives of Native Americans were changed by the explorers.

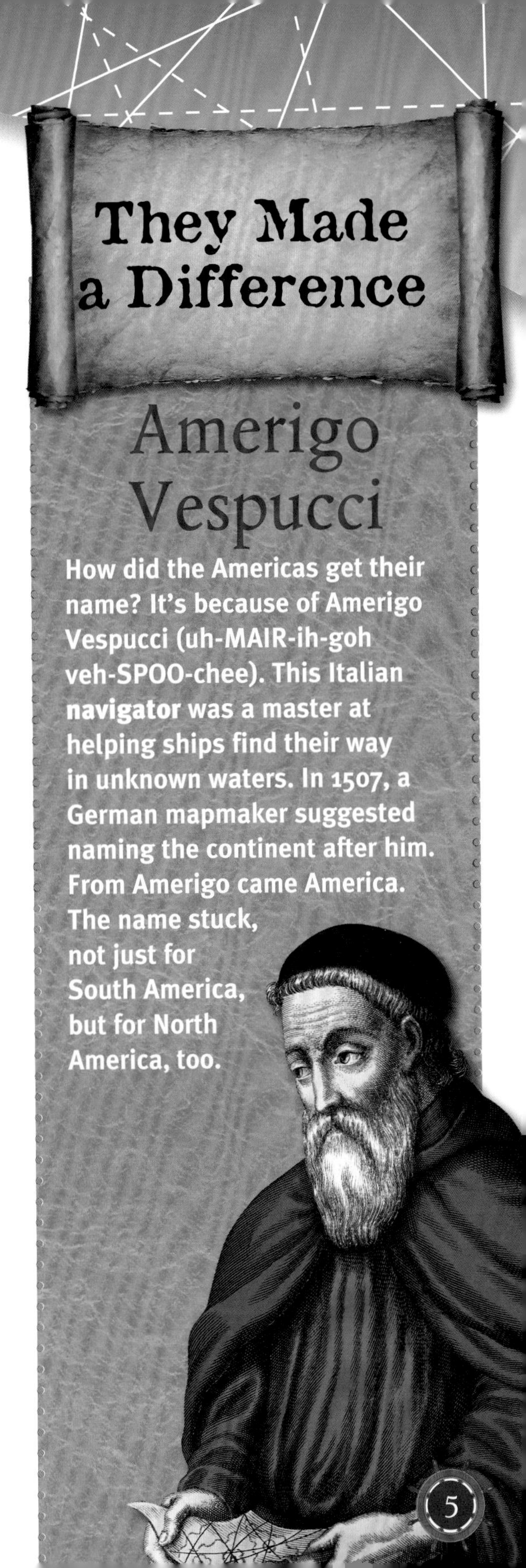

They Made a Difference

Amerigo Vespucci

How did the Americas get their name? It's because of Amerigo Vespucci (uh-MAIR-ih-goh veh-SPOO-chee). This Italian navigator was a master at helping ships find their way in unknown waters. In 1507, a German mapmaker suggested naming the continent after him. From Amerigo came America. The name stuck, not just for South America, but for North America, too.

CHAPTER 1

Spanish Explorers

New Lands and Gold for Spain

▲ The conquistadors used Hispaniola as a base to explore further into the New World.

The Spanish explorers who came after Columbus were called **conquistadors** (kahn-KEES-tuh-dorz). These brave, tough, and often cruel men didn't just explore. They seized land and conquered the people living there.

By 1496, Columbus's brother had established a **colony**, or permanent settlement, on the island of Hispaniola (his-puh-NYOH-luh). Today, the countries of Haiti and the Dominican Republic are located on Hispaniola.

The conquistadors used the colony as a base of operation. From there they captured Cuba. Then they headed toward the South American coast and across the Gulf of Mexico.

Hernán Cortés

The conquistador Hernán Cortés (air-NAHN kor-TEZ) arrived in Hispaniola in 1504. He dreamed of making his fortune. In 1511, he helped conquer Cuba's native population. And in 1519, Cuba's Spanish governor made him leader of an **expedition**, or organized trip. Cortés's job was to go to Mexico and find gold.

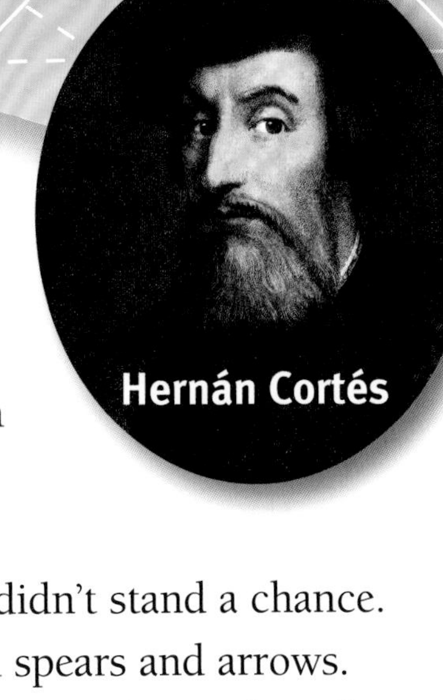
Hernán Cortés

Explorers had reached the coast of Mexico two years before. They saw people wearing gold jewelry and precious jewels. These people told of a kingdom deep in the heart of Mexico. Cortés wanted to find it.

In February of 1519, Cortés set sail with 600 men and fifteen horses in eleven ships. They landed on the mainland of Mexico. Cortés and his men battled Native American villagers. The villagers didn't stand a chance. They had spears and arrows. The Spanish had swords and guns. And, most frightening of all, the Spanish could fight from horseback.

Primary Source

Bernal Díaz (bair-NAHL DEE-ahs), a soldier who traveled with Cortés, wrote about the battle. "The Indians thought at that time that the horse and rider were one creature, for they had never seen a horse before."

In April, Cortés landed at a spot he named Veracruz. Now he was in the land of Montezuma (mahn-teh-ZOO-muh), the emperor of the Aztec Empire. This was the kingdom he was looking for. Cortés burned his ships. He didn't want any of his soldiers returning to Cuba. They were here to fight the Aztecs.

The Aztec Empire stretched across central Mexico. The Aztecs were skilled warriors. All men served as soldiers. The Aztecs were talented builders. They knew about math and astronomy, the study of the skies. They worshiped a sun god and sacrificed, or killed, their enemies to honor him.

In Tenochtitlán (tay-nahch-teet-LAHN), the Aztec capital, Montezuma was told of the Spaniards' arrival.

The Legend of Quetzalcoatl

Montezuma, like most Aztecs, believed in a powerful god named Quetzalcoatl (ket-sul-kuh-WAH-tul). The legend said that Quetzalcoatl had been driven away across the sea but was supposed to return that year. When he did, he would appear with light skin and a beard. Cortés arrived from the sea. He and his men were light-skinned and bearded. Montezuma thought Cortés just might be Quetzalcoatl.

Quetzalcoatl was shown with bright red and green feathers, similar to the feathers of the quetzal (KET-sul) bird. This bird is found in Central America.

Montezuma sent messengers to Veracruz with huge gifts of gold for Cortés. The Aztec emperor hoped that Cortés would take the gold and leave. Instead, Cortés became more determined to reach Tenochtitlán.

Cortés began a long march toward the capital. The road twisted and turned through the mountains. It passed through areas where different tribes lived. Some of the tribes fought Cortés's soldiers. But many became Cortés's allies, or friends. The Aztecs had many enemies because they were such harsh rulers. People were tired of paying taxes. They didn't want to send any more men and women to be sacrificed.

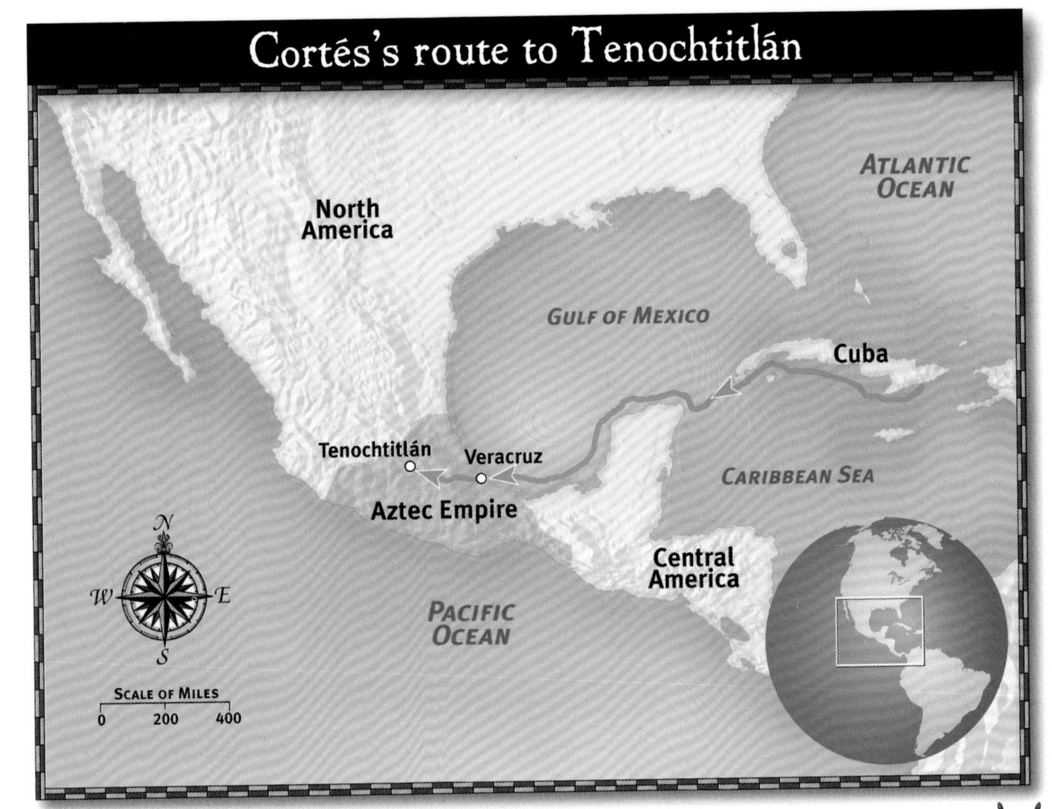

▲ **At the battle for Tenochtitlán, Spanish soldiers dressed in armor and used Spanish muskets, or rifles.**

When Cortés reached the capital, Montezuma welcomed him. The Aztec ruler showered the Spaniards with gifts. He treated them like kings.

Tenochtitlán amazed the Spaniards. The city was built on an island in the middle of a huge lake. It had temples, palaces, and towering pyramids. Tenochtitlán was home to more than 200,000 people.

Cortés put Montezuma in jail and took control of the city. He melted down the ruler's gold and silver, turning it into bars to bring back to Spain.

Eventually, the Aztecs rebelled and chased the Spaniards out of Tenochtitlán. Montezuma died in the rebellion.

Cortés didn't give up. A year later, he returned with

more troops, both Spanish and Native American. The fighting was fierce, but the Spaniards and their allies won. The Aztec Empire was finished. Their capital was in ruins. Cortés founded Mexico City on the same site. From there, the Spanish spread out through Central America.

Francisco Pizarro

The conquistadors also explored South America. The most important to do so was Francisco Pizarro (puh-ZAR-oh). Like Cortés, Pizarro heard rumors of gold.

In the 1520s, Pizarro made several voyages down the Pacific coast of South America. He met Native Americans who spoke of a great empire. It was the Inca Empire of Peru.

In 1531, Pizarro set sail to find this empire. He hoped to copy Cortés's success and find gold and fame for himself.

It's a Fact

In 1513, Pizarro completed a journey with Vasco Núñez de Balboa (VAHS-koh NOON-nyez DUH bal-BOH-uh) across the width of Central America. They became the first Europeans to see the Pacific Ocean from the west coast of the Americas.

Pizarro's expedition was smaller than that of Cortés. He took fewer than 200 men. He sailed down the coast, landed, and then left his ships behind. Pizarro and his men headed inland and then south. They marched through swampland and forests. They marched into the empire of the Incas.

The Inca Empire stretched for 2,500 miles down the great Andes Mountains in South America. At the time, it was one of the greatest empires on Earth.

A network of bridges and more than 10,000 miles of paved roads connected the empire. These "highways" passed through mountains, forests, and deserts.

Most Inca were farmers. It was hard to farm in the Andes. To do so, Inca farmers planted their crops on flat areas called terraces that they cut into the mountainsides.

Like the Aztecs, the Incas worshipped the sun. And, as Pizarro hoped, the Incas had plenty of gold. Inca rulers prized it for its beauty.

Pizarro's route

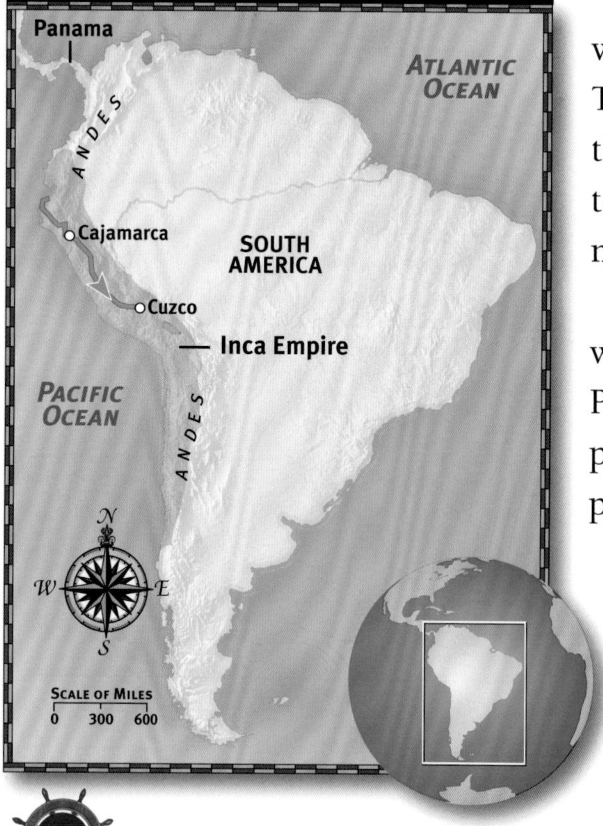

Panama
ATLANTIC OCEAN
ANDES
Cajamarca
SOUTH AMERICA
Cuzco
Inca Empire
PACIFIC OCEAN
ANDES
N
W
E
S
SCALE OF MILES
0 300 600

Over a period of many months, Pizarro and his men advanced into the empire. They learned that the Incas had just ended a brutal civil war. The two sons of the last emperor had been fighting each other for the Inca throne. The son named Atahualpa (ah-tuh-WAHL-puh) finally won. The new Inca ruler moved to the Inca city of Cajamarca (kah-huh-MAR-kah).

Pizarro and his men headed for Cajamarca. On the way, they met messengers from Atahualpa.

The two sides exchanged gifts. Pizarro told Atahualpa's men that the Spaniards were coming to help. They were invited into the city.

Once they arrived, Pizarro and his men ambushed, or surprised, Atahualpa's soldiers. They took the ruler prisoner. Atahualpa offered Pizarro a ransom if the Spaniard would let him go. The offer was huge: a room full of gold and a greater amount of silver. Pizarro accepted the offer.

It's a Fact

The room Atahualpa filled with gold and silver was huge. It was 22 feet long by 17 feet wide.

Very little of the Inca's fine gold work has survived. The Spanish melted most of it down into bars and coins.

It took months for all the gold and silver to be brought to Cajamarca. When the treasure was all there, the Spaniards melted it down. But they didn't release the Inca ruler. They strangled him. After this treacherous victory, the Spaniards marched 700 miles toward Cuzco, the Inca capital. On November 15, 1533, they entered and took over the city. Though some Incas continued to resist, the empire was finished. Now it belonged to Spain.

Deadly Diseases

The conquistadors were cruel to both the Aztecs and the Incas. But European diseases were deadlier for Native Americans than European swords and guns. When the Spaniards and other Europeans arrived in the Americas, they brought diseases like smallpox with them. These diseases were completely new to the Americas. They swept quickly from person to person.

The amount of suffering these diseases caused is hard to believe. About 30 million people lived in Mexico when Cortés arrived. About forty years later, ninety percent of them had died. The death toll from disease was similar throughout the Americas.

Solve This

1. **How many Native Americans were living in Mexico forty years after Cortés arrived?**

More Spanish Explorations

In 1513, Juan Ponce de Leon (PAHN-suh DAY LEE-one) set sail from Puerto Rico to find land to the north. Two weeks later, he sighted the territory he named Florida.

Ponce de Leon

In 1528, Alvar Núñez Cabeza de Vaca (AL-var NOON-nyez kuh-BAY-suh DUH VAH-kuh) became shipwrecked on what is now the Texas coast. He spent the next eight years wandering and exploring. He walked through what are now Texas and the Southwest before reaching Spanish settlements in Mexico.

Hernando De Soto

Hernando De Soto (air-NAHN-doh DUH SOH-toh) hoped to find an Inca-like empire in Florida. In 1539, he landed on the Florida coast and led 600 men on a difficult journey across today's southeast United States. He found no empire, but he became the first European to reach the Mississippi River.

In 1540, Francisco Vásquez de Coronado (frun-SIS-koh VAHS-kez DUH kor-uh-NAH-doh) headed out of Mexico into what we now know as Arizona, New Mexico, and northern Texas. Coronado hoped to find cities of gold. Instead, he and his men found pueblo-dwelling Indians like the Hopi and the Zuni. Coronado failed to find cities of gold, but he and his men became the first Europeans to see the American buffalo.

English and Dutch Explorers

The Search for a Northwest Passage

Spain was growing rich from its New World explorations. This made other European countries such as England, France, and Holland jealous. These countries began sending out explorers of their own. They wanted to claim a share of the New World.

These countries also wanted to find the sea route to Asia. They thought perhaps it lay to the north of the area explored by Spain—a northwest passage.

John Cabot ▶

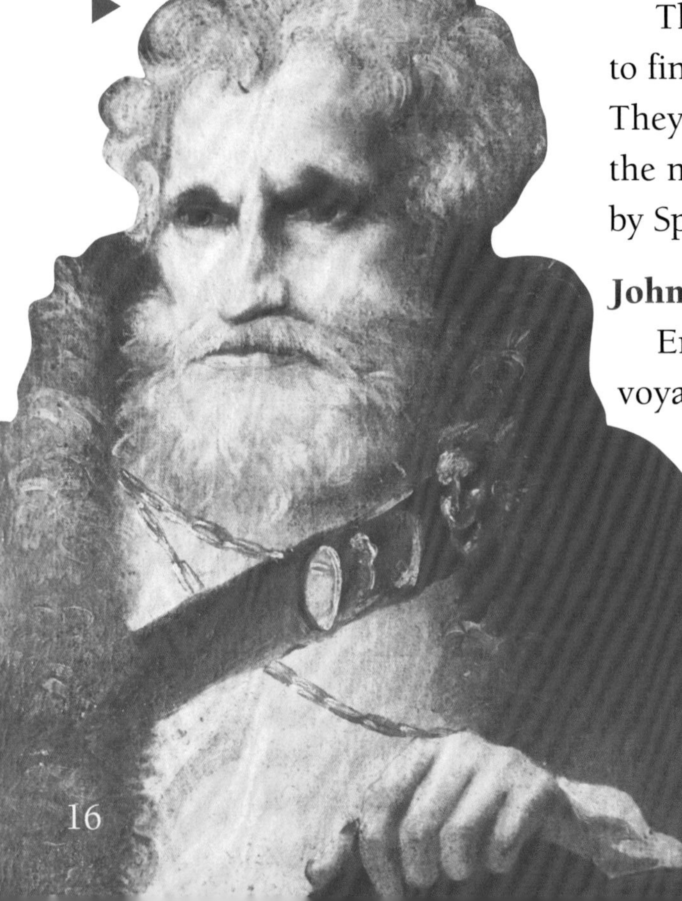

John Cabot

England's first important voyage began five years after Columbus reached the Americas. In May 1497, explorer John Cabot set sail from England in a small ship. He had a crew of less than twenty men.

John Cabot explains his voyage to King Henry VII.

Cabot was from Venice, Italy. His Italian name was Caboto (kuh-BOH-toh). Yet he was working for England's King Henry VII. The English had a special interest in a sea route to Asia. Asian goods were especially costly in England. That was because of England's location. It lay farther west from Asia than other European countries.

Cabot's plan for finding a sea route was different from that of Columbus. Cabot was going to sail further north. Since Earth was curved, Cabot figured this route would be shorter and faster. So after leaving England, he sailed north to Ireland. Then he turned west to cross the Atlantic Ocean.

Primary Source

King Henry VII gave John Cabot a royal decree, or official order. This order gave Cabot "full and free authority, leave, and power to sail to all parts, countryes, and seas of the East, of the West, and of the North . . . to seek out, discover, and finde whatsoever isles, countreyes, regions, or provinces . . . which before this time have bene unknowen . . ."

Cabot's own account of the trip was lost. Historians have pieced together what probably happened. After thirty-three days in the open sea, Cabot and his crew saw land. It was probably the cliffs of Newfoundland, a large island off Canada's eastern shore. They made a landing. In doing so, they became the first English and Italians to set foot in North America. Cabot claimed the land for Henry VII and spent a few weeks exploring the area. Then he turned around and headed back to England.

The return trip was faster. With the help of the wind and ocean currents, it took about fifteen days. When his ship landed, Cabot raced to London on horseback. He told the king what he had found. He described the lands he had claimed for England. He

Solve This

2. Cabot's return trip across the Atlantic took 15 days. The distance was about 1,725 nautical miles. On average, how many nautical miles did Cabot's ship travel each day on the return trip?

mistakenly said the lands were the tip of Asia. He described fishing grounds jumping with fish.

Cabot had not found spices or gold, but the king was still thrilled. If this was the tip of Asia, the rest must be near! He agreed to a second, larger expedition.

In 1498, Cabot set sail again, this time with five ships. One ship turned back soon after sailing. The other four ships, and Cabot, were never seen again. Like Columbus, Cabot died thinking he had landed in Asia. He had not, but he had made England's first claim in the New World.

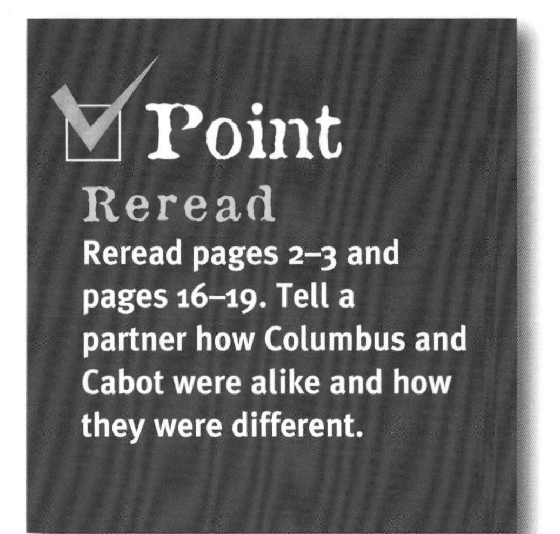

Point

Reread

Reread pages 2–3 and pages 16–19. Tell a partner how Columbus and Cabot were alike and how they were different.

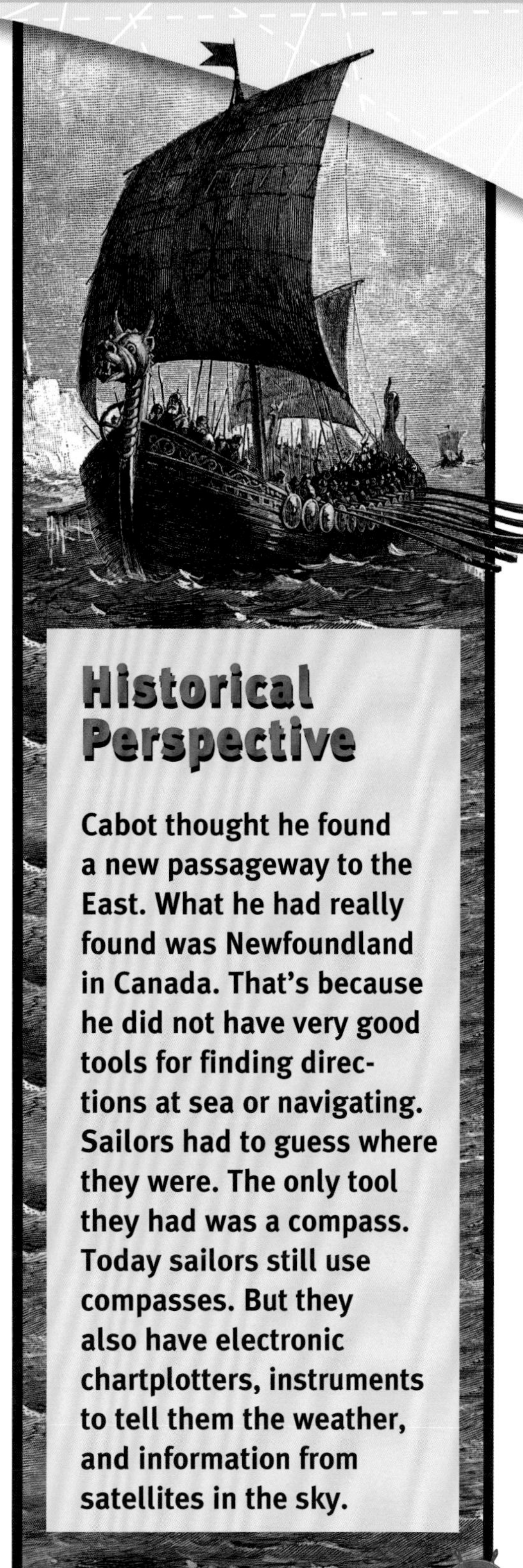

Historical Perspective

Cabot thought he found a new passageway to the East. What he had really found was Newfoundland in Canada. That's because he did not have very good tools for finding directions at sea or navigating. Sailors had to guess where they were. The only tool they had was a compass. Today sailors still use compasses. But they also have electronic chartplotters, instruments to tell them the weather, and information from satellites in the sky.

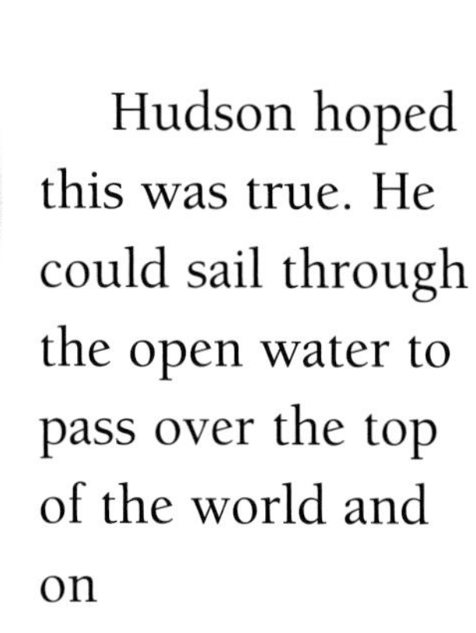

Henry Hudson

When Cabot disappeared, the English lost interest in finding a northwest passage to Asia. More than one hundred years passed before another English navigator searched for a northwest passage. In 1607, Henry Hudson set out to find a passage to Asia through the North Pole.

In 1607, no one had been to the North Pole. Scientists then knew the North Pole got constant sunshine in the summer. They probably believed that the sun melted enough ice to create a stretch of open water. If that was so, a ship could sail through this passage.

Hudson hoped this was true. He could sail through the open water to pass over the top of the world and on to Asia.

But Hudson was unsuccessful. Time and again, towering walls of ice stopped his ships. After three months, he gave up. He had gone farther north than any explorer before him.

▼ Iceberg-filled waters forced Hudson to turn back.

Hudson tried again the next year. This time, he headed northeast. He sailed past the coast of Norway. He wanted to continue to Asia through the cold waters north of Russia.

The seas were very rough, fog-covered, and filled with chunks of ice. Again, Hudson's way was blocked. But instead of returning to England, he headed toward the New World.

But his crew had had enough. They threatened to **mutiny**, or rebel. Hudson gave in and pointed the ship back home.

After this failure, English businessmen didn't want to pay for another voyage by Hudson. But Hudson didn't give up. He turned to England's rivals, France and Holland.

▲ Sailors mutiny against their captain.

Primary Source

During the sixteenth and seventeenth centuries, sailors would often mutiny on the long, difficult sailing journeys. The men wanted to be home. They were tired of pickled meat and stale biscuits, called "hardtack." One sixteenth-century sailor wrote ". . . our ship biscuits had become so wormy that, God help me, I saw many who waited for darkeness . . . that they might not see the maggots; and others were so used to eating them that they didn't even trouble to pick them out . . ."

In 1609, Hudson was hired by Holland to search to the northeast. At first he headed in that direction, but then he turned west toward the New World. This time he made it. On what is now the coast of Maine, Hudson and his crew met Native Americans.

At first, the meeting was peaceful. Hudson traded tools and beads for valuable beaver and fox fur. But then Hudson's men attacked the Native Americans and robbed them of their goods. Before the Indians could react, Hudson sailed away.

Hudson continued to explore. He reached the mouth of a mighty river. Today that river is known as the Hudson River. He followed the river upstream, believing it might be the Northwest Passage. It was not. When the river grew too shallow, Hudson turned back.

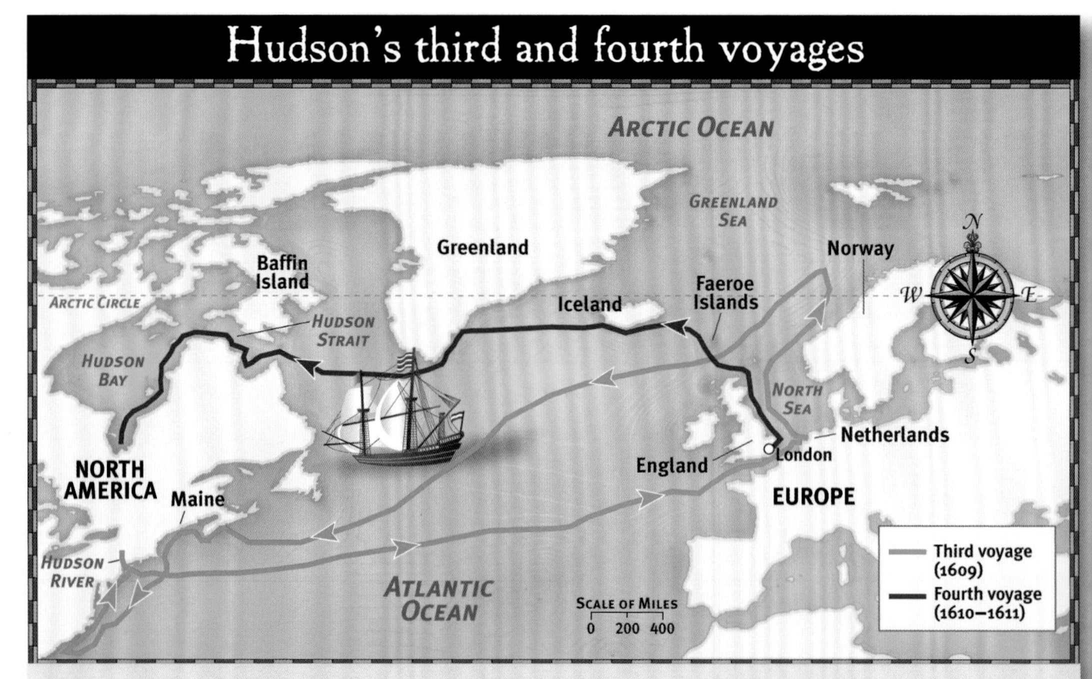

▲ **On these voyages, Hudson explored the coast along the Atlantic Ocean from what is now Maine to South Carolina.**

Hudson made one last journey. This time the English hired him. He sailed along Canada's coast and down into a huge, open body of water now known as the Hudson Bay.

The crew ran short of food. After a difficult winter, they wanted to go back home. Hudson refused. The men mutinied and took control. They placed Hudson in a small boat and left him in the Hudson Bay. He was never seen again.

Hudson never found a northwest passage. However, England and Holland learned about North America from his journeys. In 1624, people from Holland settled by the mouth of the Hudson River. That settlement became the city of New York.

▼ **engraving of Henry Hudson's last voyage**

French Explorers

A French Foothold in the New World

Like England and Holland, France wanted to catch up with Spain in the New World. And France also hoped to find a sea route to Asia.

Jacques Cartier

The explorer whom France turned to was Jacques Cartier (ZHAHK KAR-tee-ay).

Jacques Cartier

As a young man, Cartier had sailed to the fishing grounds off the coast of Newfoundland. He had years of experience at sea. He was a skilled navigator.

In April of 1534, Cartier left France. He sailed past Newfoundland in twenty days. He continued to sail along the coast of North America, searching for a northwest passage. Wherever he landed, he claimed the land for France. He met the Native Americans who lived in the region. These were the Huron and the Micmac (MIK-mak) tribes. They made their living fishing and trapping animals.

Cartier took two of the natives back with him to France. It may have been by force. These natives were sons of a Huron chief.

The natives told Cartier about an endless river that led to wealthy kingdoms. Cartier was filled with wonder. He hoped he would find gold and silver, like the Spanish explorers. He also hoped that this endless river might be the Northwest Passage. So in 1535, Cartier set out from France again. He crossed the Atlantic and headed for the river. When he found it, he named it the St. Lawrence.

Cartier sailed as far as he could. Then he came to a set of dangerous rapids. It was not possible to pass through these rough waters by boat, so he stopped. Cartier found no riches, but he did meet many Native Americans who lived on the St. Lawrence River. He spent a tough, cold winter along the river. Then he returned to France. With him were several Native Americans he had captured, including the Huron chief.

It's a Fact

Cartier named the country of Canada after the Huron village Kanata.

▲ On his second voyage, Cartier explored far up the St. Lawrence River.

In 1541, Cartier made a final voyage. His goal was to create a colony. The project was a failure. The winter was terrible, and Native Americans attacked the settlement. Cartier spent his time in a fruitless search for gold and jewels before returning to France.

Still, Cartier's voyages were very important. France now claimed large amounts of land in the New World. Cartier found a water route that led deep into the North American continent. And he had met Native Americans who lived there.

Samuel de Champlain

For a half century after Cartier's colony failed, few Frenchman came to live in the New World. That changed, beginning in the early seventeenth century, thanks to Samuel de Champlain (DUH sham-PLANE).

▲ Cartier sailed up the St. Lawrence River to a spot where the city of Montreal, Canada, stands today.

Champlain had already been to North America. In 1608, he led a voyage of his own. He followed Cartier's route and founded a trading post on the St. Lawrence River. This became the city of Quebec (kwih-BEK), the oldest city in Canada.

At the trading post, Champlain traded French goods like cloth and tools for furs with local Indians. Champlain wanted to build good relations with the Native Americans.

▲ Champlain learned the language of the Huron Indians and respected their ways.

Solve This

3. Use the graph to answer this question: How many French people lived in New France when Champlain arrived in 1608?

a. less than 1,500
b. between 1,500 and 2,500
c. close to 10,000

French Population of New France

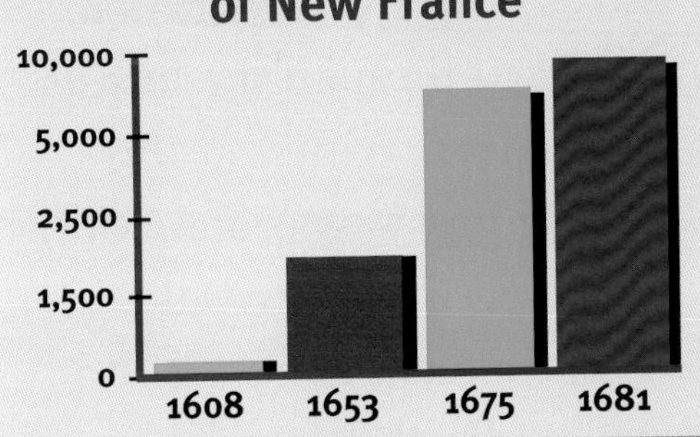

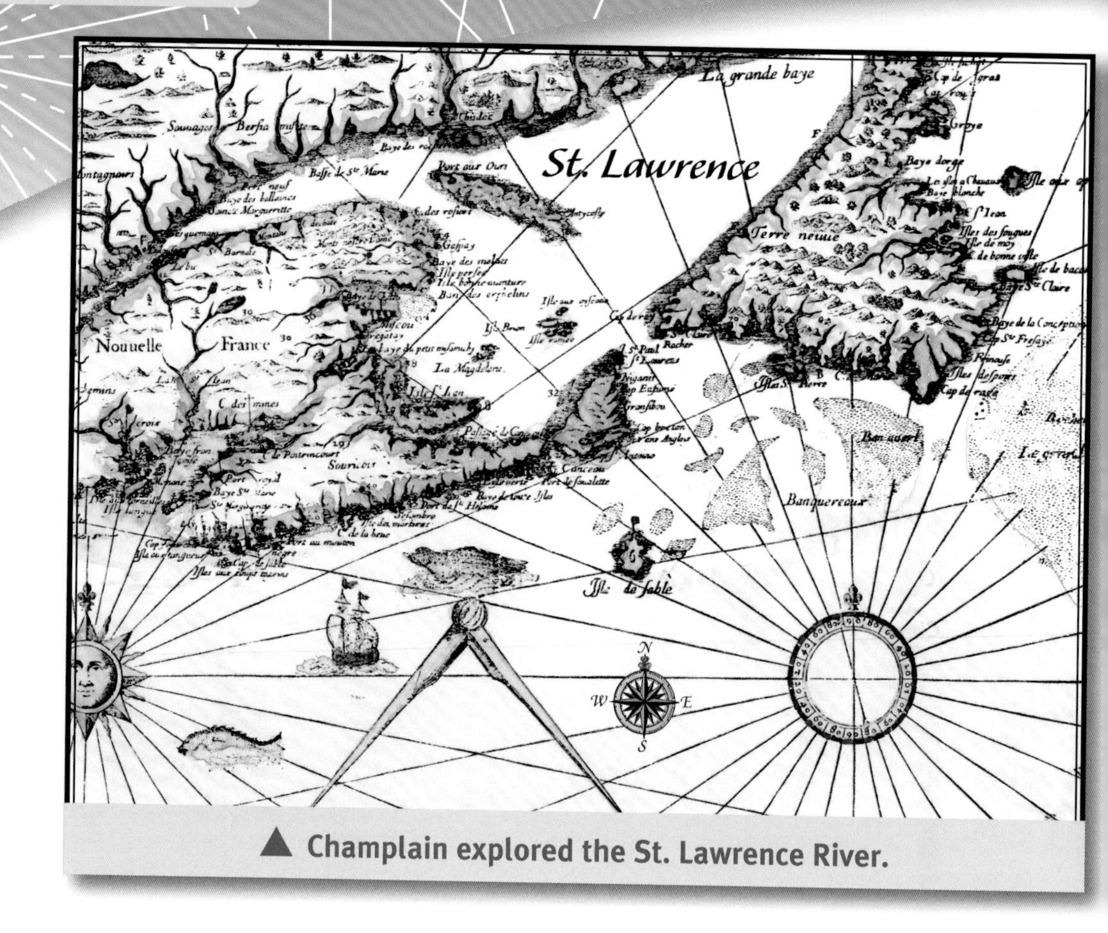

▲ Champlain explored the St. Lawrence River.

Champlain became friends with the Algonquin (al-GAHN-kwin) and Huron Indians. He explored and mapped the region. He traveled up rivers by canoe. He hiked through the forests and valleys. Winter at the trading post was brutal. More men died than survived.

Champlain continued to explore for the next six years. He went past the rapids that had stopped Cartier. He discovered Lake Huron, the Great Lake deep inside North America. He helped his friends, the Algonquin and Huron Indians, fight against their enemy, the Iroquois (EER-uh-kwoi). Because of this, the Iroquois would be an enemy of French colonists for years to come.

Champlain spent the next twenty years traveling back and forth between "Old France" and "New France." The explorer became a colony builder. He helped organize the fur trade. He helped get settlers to move to New France. He gathered money to build up the new French colonies.

In 1633, Champlain returned to New France permanently. He became governor of the colony. When he died there two years later, many thought of him as the "Father of New France."

▲ The Hurons helped the French increase their fur-trading business. They were allies with the French for many years.

Conclusion

A great age of exploration began with Columbus. Explorers searched for trade routes, for new lands, and for silver and gold. When the Age of Exploration was over, the world was a very different place. European countries had gained huge amounts of territory. They had built colonies in North and South America. Their banks were filled with bars of gold from the New World.

For Native Americans, the changes were far less positive. Many had died from European diseases. Others had been enslaved. Still more would be pushed from their land as more European settlers arrived.

The Age of Exploration lasted just over a century. The voyages of explorers such as Columbus, Cabot, Cortés, and Hudson had changed the world forever.

Glossary

colony (KAH-luh-nee) an area settled by people from another country (page 6)

conquistador (kahn-KEES-tuh-dor) a Spanish soldier who explored and conquered Native Americans in Mexico, Central, and South America (page 6)

continent (KAHN-tih-nent) one of seven large land masses that make up Earth (page 3)

expedition (ek-speh-DIH-shun) a long journey with a particular goal or mission (page 6)

mutiny (MYOO-tih-nee) to rebel against or disobey the captain of a ship (page 21)

navigator (NA-vih-gay-ter) sailor in charge of finding direction for a ship (page 5)

nomad (NOH-mad) a member of a group of people who wander from place to place (page 4)

port (PORT) a harbor where ships come to anchor safely and load and unload goods (page 3)

route (ROOT or ROWT) a path you follow to get from one place to another (page 2)

Solve This

Answers

1. **Page 14:** 3 million
2. **Page 18:** 115 nautical miles
3. **Page 27:** less than 1,500

Index